21 DAYS OF
PRAYER
THAT ACTIVATE
DIVINE
BLESSINGS

MAYOR CLEMENT &
SOULFUL GRACE

21 Days of Prayer that Activate Divine Blessings

Copyright © 2024
Christ Glory Interpreters

ISBN:
9798327361157

Imprint:
Independently published

Contents

Acknowledgment

We are deeply grateful to everyone who contributed to the creation of this book, **21 Days of Prayer that Activate Divine Blessings**.

First and foremost, we thank God for His divine inspiration and guidance throughout this journey.

To our families, thank you for your unwavering support, love, and patience. Your prayers and encouragement have been invaluable.

We extend our heartfelt thanks to our team of editors, proofreaders, and designers, whose expertise and dedication have shaped this book. A special thank you to our publisher for bringing this project to life.

To our readers, thank you for seeking to deepen your spiritual journey. We hope these prayers inspire and uplift you.

Finally, a profound thank you to my co-author, Soulful Grace. Your wisdom and partnership have been a blessing.
May these prayers guide you towards a life filled with divine blessings.

Introduction

Welcome to **21 Days of Prayer that Activate Divine Blessing**. This book is a labor of love and faith, designed to guide you through a spiritual journey where you can experience the fullness of God's blessings in every area of your life. As we embark on this journey together, it is my prayer that you will encounter God in profound and life-changing ways.

The Importance of This Book's Title

The title of this book is not just a collection of words; it is a declaration of faith and purpose. Each day, for 21 days, we will focus on prayers that are specifically crafted to activate God's blessings. The number 21 is significant because it represents a period of transformation and breakthrough. Daniel fasted and prayed for 21 days, seeking understanding from God, and his prayers were answered (Daniel 10:2-14). This book draws on that biblical precedent, inviting you to dedicate 21 days to focused, intentional prayer.

Why "Prayer"?

Prayer is our direct line of communication with God. It is through prayer that we express our deepest desires, seek guidance, and align our will with God's. Jesus himself emphasized the power of prayer, teaching us to pray with faith and persistence (Luke 11:9-10). This book will guide you in praying with a purpose, expecting that God will hear and respond.

Why "Activate"?

To activate means to make something active or operative. In the context of this book, it means putting our faith into action. James 2:17 tells us that faith without works is dead. By engaging in these prayers, you are actively participating in God's promises and positioning yourself to receive His blessings. Activation requires intentionality and commitment, and that's what this book is all about.

Why "Divine Blessing"?

Divine blessings are those that come directly from God. They are not just material or financial; they encompass every aspect of our lives—spiritual, emotional, physical, and relational. Ephesians 1:3 says that God has blessed us with every spiritual blessing in Christ. This book aims to help you recognize and claim those blessings, living a life that reflects God's abundance and favor.

What to Expect in This Book

This book is divided into 21 chapters, each focusing on a specific area where you can seek and activate God's blessings. We begin by understanding what it means to be blessed by God, exploring biblical definitions and examples. You will learn to pray for and experience God's favor in every aspect of your life, from personal relationships to professional endeavors. The chapters will guide you in praying for blessings in your relationships, financial provision, physical healing, and wellness, emphasizing that God cares about every part of your life. You will also seek God's guidance and favor in your career or business, and for those involved in ministry, we provide prayers for God's anointing and fruitfulness.

Throughout the book, we highlight the connection between obedience and blessing, learning biblical principles of giving and generosity, and praying for community unity and prosperity. Protection is a key area, seeking God's promises to keep you safe, along with praying for covenant blessings, inner peace, and emotional well-being. We also guide you in prayers for restoration if you have experienced loss or brokenness. You will seek God's wisdom in decision-making, generational blessings, and cultivate a heart of gratitude. In times of adversity, you will learn to pray for strength and trust in God's faithfulness. The journey concludes with prayers for divine intervention, abundant harvest, and an outpouring of God's love in your life.

Key Points to Remember

- **Prayer is Powerful**: Jesus taught us to pray persistently and with faith. Prayer is not just a ritual; it is a powerful tool for change.

- **Blessings are Multifaceted**: God's blessings are not limited to material wealth. They include spiritual, emotional, relational, and physical aspects.

- **Activation Requires Faith and Action**: To activate divine blessings, you must pray with faith and take actions that align with God's will.

How to Use This Book

- **Dedicate Time Daily**: Set aside a specific time each day to read and pray. Consistency is key to experiencing the full impact of these prayers.

- **Reflect on Scripture**: Each chapter includes Bible references. Take time to read and meditate on these verses, letting God's Word deepen your understanding.

- **Journal Your Journey**: Keep a journal of your prayers and the ways God responds. This will help you see His faithfulness and growth in your spiritual life.

- **Share Your Experience**: Consider praying with a friend or small group. Sharing this journey with others can provide encouragement and accountability.

As you embark on this 21-day journey of prayer, my prayer for you is that you will experience God's presence in new and powerful ways. May you be filled with His peace, guided by His wisdom, and surrounded by His love. May these prayers activate divine blessings in your life, bringing you closer to the abundant life that God desires for you.

Remember, God is faithful. As you seek Him, He will meet you. As you pray, He will hear you. And as you activate these divine blessings, your life will be a testimony of His goodness and grace.

Day 1

Prayer for Understanding Divine Blessing

Understanding divine blessing is the first step to living a life filled with God's favor and abundance. A divine blessing is more than just material wealth; it encompasses every aspect of our lives—spiritual, emotional, physical, and relational. When we understand what it means to be blessed by God, we align ourselves with His will and open our hearts to receive His countless blessings.

God's blessings are promises that He has given us through His Word, and as we seek to understand them, we grow in faith and gratitude. The Bible says, *"The Lord bless you and keep you; the Lord make his face shine on you and be gracious to you" (Numbers 6:24-25).* This understanding helps us to live with confidence, knowing that God's favor surrounds us like a shield *(Psalm 5:12).*

Jesus taught us the importance of seeking righteousness, saying, *"Blessed are those who hunger and thirst for righteousness, for they will be filled" (Matthew 5:6).* As we hunger for understanding His blessings, we position ourselves to receive the fullness of His grace. Furthermore, *Proverbs 10:22* reminds us, *"The blessing of the Lord brings wealth, without painful toil for it."* When we comprehend this, we can trust in God's provision without anxiety. Let's commit today to understanding and embracing the divine blessings God has for us.

Prayer Points

1. Lord, I thank You for Your promise of blessings. Open my heart to understand and receive Your divine blessings, in Jesus' name.

2. Father, teach me to recognize and appreciate the blessings You have already placed in my life, in Jesus' name.

3. Lord, grant me wisdom and discernment to seek Your blessings in every area of my life, in Jesus' name.

4. Heavenly Father, help me to align my desires with Your will, so that I may walk in Your blessings daily, in Jesus' name.

5. Lord, bless my mind with the understanding of Your Word, so that I may live according to Your promises, in Jesus' name.

6. Father, bless my spirit with faith and trust in Your plans for my life, in Jesus' name.

7. Lord, bless my relationships, that they may reflect Your love and grace, in Jesus' name.

8. Father, bless my endeavors and efforts, so that they may prosper and bring glory to Your name, in Jesus' name.

9. Lord, bless my body with health and strength, that I may serve You with all my might, in Jesus' name.

10. Father, bless my finances, that I may use them wisely and generously for Your kingdom, in Jesus' name.

11. Lord, bless my heart with peace and joy, even in the midst of challenges, in Jesus' name.

12. Father, bless my journey of faith, that I may grow closer to You and be a blessing to others, in Jesus' name.

Affirmation

Father, I affirm today that I am blessed by You in every way. Your favor surrounds me, Your wisdom guides me, and Your love sustains me. I am grateful for Your blessings and commit to living a life that reflects Your grace and goodness. In Jesus' name, Amen.

Day 2

Prayer for Activating God's Favor

God's favor is a powerful force in our lives, opening doors that no man can shut and bringing blessings that we could never achieve on our own. When we activate God's favor, we position ourselves to receive His grace in every area of our lives.

Favor is not something we can earn; it is a gift from God, given to those who seek Him with a sincere heart. The Bible tells us, **"For you bless the righteous, O Lord; you cover him with favor as with a shield" (Psalm 5:12).** Understanding and activating this favor can transform our lives, bringing us into alignment with God's will and purpose.

Favor is evident throughout the Bible. For instance, Joseph found favor in the eyes of Pharaoh and was elevated to a position of power *(Genesis 39:4)*. Mary, the mother of Jesus, was highly favored by God and chosen for a unique and holy purpose *(Luke 1:28)*. Jesus Himself grew in favor with God and man *(Luke 2:52)*.

As we seek to activate God's favor in our lives, we can expect similar transformations, opportunities, and blessings. Today, let's pray fervently for the activation of God's favor in every aspect of our lives.

Prayer Points

1. Lord, I thank You for Your favor that surrounds me like a shield. Help me to recognize and activate this favor in my life, in Jesus' name.

2. Father, grant me favor in the eyes of those I interact with today, that Your name may be glorified through my actions, in Jesus' name.

3. Lord, bless me with Your favor in my workplace, that I may find success and advancement according to Your will, in Jesus' name.

4. Father, let Your favor open doors of opportunity that have been closed, and grant me the wisdom to walk through them, in Jesus' name.

5. Lord, bless my relationships with favor, bringing harmony and understanding, in Jesus' name.

6. Father, bless my family with Your favor, that we may live in unity and love, in Jesus' name.

7. Lord, grant me favor in my financial endeavors, providing for my needs and enabling me to bless others, in Jesus' name.

8. Father, let Your favor rest upon my ministry, that I may effectively share Your love and truth, in Jesus' name.

9. Lord, bless me with favor in my studies and learning, granting me understanding and success, in Jesus' name.

10. Father, let Your favor be evident in my health, granting me strength and vitality, in Jesus' name.

11. Lord, bless me with favor in every decision I make, guiding me with Your wisdom and discernment, in Jesus' name.

12. Father, grant me favor with those in authority, that I may influence positive change for Your kingdom, in Jesus' name.

Affirmation

Father, I affirm today that Your favor is upon me. Your grace goes before me, opening doors and creating opportunities. I am surrounded by Your love and guided by Your wisdom. I walk in the assurance of Your favor, knowing that You are with me in every step I take. In Jesus' name, Amen.

Day 3

Prayer for Blessings in Relationships

Relationships are a fundamental part of our lives, and God's desire is for us to be blessed in our interactions with others. Healthy, loving relationships reflect His nature and bring joy and fulfillment to our lives. When we seek God's blessings in our relationships, we invite His love, peace, and harmony into our connections with family, friends, and colleagues.

The Bible says, *"Two are better than one because they have a good return for their labor" (Ecclesiastes 4:9).* This highlights the importance of supportive and blessed relationships in our lives.

God's Word is filled with examples of blessed relationships. David and Jonathan shared a deep, loyal friendship that was a source of strength and encouragement *(1 Samuel 18:1-4).* Ruth and Naomi's relationship showcased the beauty of commitment and support in difficult times (*Ruth 1:16-17).*

Jesus Himself emphasized the importance of love in relationships, saying, *"A new command I give you: Love one another. As I have loved you, so you must love one another" (John 13:34).* As we pray for blessings in our relationships, let's seek

God's guidance and favor, asking Him to strengthen and enrich every connection in our lives.

Prayer Points

1. Lord, I thank You for the relationships You have blessed me with. Help me to nurture and cherish them, in Jesus' name.

2. Father, bless my relationship with my family, filling our home with love, peace, and understanding, in Jesus' name.

3. Lord, grant me favor in my friendships, that they may be sources of encouragement and joy, in Jesus' name.

4. Father, bless my marriage (or future marriage) with unity and love, reflecting Your relationship with the church, in Jesus' name.

5. Lord, help me to forgive those who have hurt me and to seek reconciliation in broken relationships, in Jesus' name.

6. Father, bless my relationship with my children (or future children), guiding me to raise them in Your ways, in Jesus' name.

7. Lord, grant me wisdom and patience in my interactions with colleagues and superiors, that I may be a blessing in my workplace, in Jesus' name.

8. Father, bless my relationship with my neighbors, fostering a spirit of community and support, in Jesus' name.

9. Lord, help me to love others as You have loved me, showing kindness and compassion in all my relationships, in Jesus' name.

10. Father, bless my relationship with my spiritual mentors and leaders, that I may grow in faith and wisdom, in Jesus' name.

11. Lord, grant me discernment in choosing my friends, that I may be surrounded by those who uplift and inspire me, in Jesus' name.

12. Father, bless my relationship with those who do not yet know You, using me as a vessel to share Your love and truth, in Jesus' name.

Affirmation

Father, I affirm today that my relationships are blessed by You. Your love flows through me, bringing peace and joy to every connection. I am surrounded by supportive, loving, and uplifting relationships. Thank You for the gift of companionship and community. In Jesus' name, Amen.

Day 4

Prayer for Financial Blessings

Financial blessings are an essential aspect of our lives, as they enable us to provide for our needs, support others, and contribute to God's work on earth. When we seek God's blessings in our finances, we acknowledge Him as our provider and trust Him to meet all our needs according to His riches in glory.

The Bible assures us, *"The blessing of the Lord brings wealth, without painful toil for it" (Proverbs 10:22)*. Therefore, as we pray for financial blessings, let us do so with faith, knowing that God desires to prosper us and bless the work of our hands.

Financial blessings are not only about accumulating wealth but also about being good stewards of what God has entrusted to us. Jesus taught us the importance of stewardship, saying, *"Give, and it will be given to you. A good measure, pressed down, shaken together and running over, will be poured into your lap. For with the measure you use, it will be measured to you" (Luke 6:38).* As we pray for financial blessings, let us also commit to being generous givers, trusting that God will bless us abundantly in return.

Prayer Points

1. Lord, I thank You for being my provider and sustainer. Bless my finances, that I may have more than enough to meet my needs and bless others, in Jesus' name.

2. Father, grant me wisdom and discipline in managing my finances, that I may be a good steward of the resources You have entrusted to me, in Jesus' name.

3. Lord, open doors of opportunity for increase and prosperity in my career or business, according to Your will and purpose for my life, in Jesus' name.

4. Father, bless the work of my hands, that I may experience abundance and success in all my endeavors, in Jesus' name.

5. Lord, help me to be debt-free and to live within my means, avoiding the traps of excessive borrowing and financial bondage, in Jesus' name.

6. Father, remove any obstacles or hindrances that may be blocking the flow of financial blessings into my life, in Jesus' name.

7. Lord, grant me favor with those who have the power to bless me financially, that they may be instruments of Your provision and blessing, in Jesus' name.

8. Father, teach me to be a cheerful giver, sowing generously into Your kingdom and the needs of others, knowing that You will multiply my seed sown, in Jesus' name.

9. Lord, bless my investments and savings, that they may grow and multiply according to Your divine plan, in Jesus' name.

10. Father, help me to trust in Your provision and not to worry about tomorrow, knowing that You are faithful to provide for all my needs, in Jesus' name.

11. Lord, give me creative ideas and strategies for generating wealth and prosperity, that I may be a channel of blessing to others, in Jesus' name.

12. Father, bless me with a spirit of contentment and gratitude, that I may be satisfied with what You have provided and not be driven by greed or covetousness, in Jesus' name.

Affirmation

Father, I affirm today that You are my provider and sustainer. I trust in Your promise to bless me abundantly and meet all my needs according to Your riches in glory. I commit to being a faithful steward of the resources You have entrusted to me, and I thank You for the financial blessings that are coming my way. In Jesus' name, Amen.

Day 5

Prayer for Health and Wellness Blessings

Health and wellness are precious blessings from God, encompassing not only physical well-being but also emotional and spiritual wholeness. Our bodies are temples of the Holy Spirit, and caring for them is a sacred responsibility. God desires for us to live healthy and vibrant lives, free from sickness and disease. The Bible affirms this truth in *3 John 1:2*, saying, *"Beloved, I pray that all may go well with you and that you may be in good health, as it goes well with your soul."* This verse underscores the importance of holistic health, where our physical and spiritual well-being are interconnected.

Our faith in God's healing power is rooted in Scripture. In *Psalm 103:2-3*, we read, *"Bless the Lord, O my soul, and forget not all his benefits, who forgives all your iniquity, who heals all your diseases."* These words remind us of God's promise to heal and restore us.

Jesus Himself performed numerous miracles of healing during His ministry on earth, demonstrating His authority over sickness and infirmity. As we pray for health and wellness blessings today, let us do so with unwavering faith, trusting in God's goodness and mercy.

Prayer Points

1. Lord, I pray for divine blessings of health and wellness to permeate every cell of my body, restoring me to wholeness and vitality, in Jesus' name.

2. Father, bless my physical body with strength and resilience, guarding me against illness and injury, in Jesus' name.

3. Lord, grant me wisdom to make healthy lifestyle choices that honor You and promote well-being, in Jesus' name.

4. Father, bless my mind with peace and clarity, free from anxiety and stress, in Jesus' name.

5. Lord, I pray for emotional healing and stability, that Your love may heal every wound and bring inner peace, in Jesus' name.

6. Father, bless my relationships with others, fostering love and support that contributes to my overall wellness, in Jesus' name.

7. Lord, I lift up to You any areas of my life where I am struggling with health issues, trusting in Your healing touch to bring restoration, in Jesus' name.

8. Father, bless the healthcare providers and caregivers who work tirelessly to support those in need, granting them strength and compassion, in Jesus' name.

9. Lord, I pray for those who are suffering from chronic illnesses or disabilities, asking for Your comfort and presence to be with them, in Jesus' name.

10. Father, bless my spiritual life with fervent faith and intimacy with You, knowing that a healthy soul is vital for overall well-being, in Jesus' name.

11. Lord, I commit to stewarding my body well, treating it with care and respect as a temple of the Holy Spirit, in Jesus' name.

12. Father, I thank You for the promise of health and wellness blessings, and I receive them with gratitude and faith, in Jesus' name.

Affirmation

Father, I affirm today that Your desire for my health and wellness is evident in Your Word and demonstrated through Your Son, Jesus Christ. I receive Your blessings of wholeness and vitality with open arms, trusting in Your faithfulness to sustain me. May my life be a testimony to Your healing power, bringing glory to Your name. In Jesus' name, Amen.

Day 6

Prayer for Career and Business Blessings

Our careers and businesses are significant aspects of our lives, through which we have the opportunity to fulfill our God-given purposes and contribute to the world around us. As believers, we are called to pursue excellence in all that we do, knowing that our work is ultimately unto the Lord.

Proverbs 16:3 reminds us, *"Commit your work to the Lord, and your plans will be established."* This verse emphasizes the importance of entrusting our careers and businesses to God, seeking His guidance and blessing in all our endeavors.

Throughout Scripture, we see God's faithfulness in providing for His people's needs, including their vocational aspirations. In *Jeremiah 29:11*, God declares, *"For I know the plans I have for you, plans for welfare and not for evil, to give you a future and a hope."* This promise assures us that God has good plans for our careers and businesses, plans that are filled with blessings and prosperity.

As we lift our prayers for career and business blessings today, let us do so with confidence, knowing that God is faithful to fulfill His promises and grant us success according to His will.

Prayer Points

1. Lord, I pray for Your blessings upon my career and business endeavors, that they may prosper and bear fruit according to Your perfect plan, in Jesus' name.

2. Father, grant me wisdom and discernment in all my professional decisions, guiding me along the path that leads to success and fulfillment, in Jesus' name.

3. Lord, bless the work of my hands and the labor of my mind, that I may excel in my chosen field and bring glory to Your name, in Jesus' name.

4. Father, open doors of opportunity for me in my career and business ventures, connecting me with the right people and resources to advance Your kingdom purposes, in Jesus' name.

5. Lord, I surrender my ambitions and aspirations to You, trusting in Your divine provision and guidance for my career and business journey, in Jesus' name.

6. Father, bless my professional relationships and interactions, that they may be characterized by integrity, honesty, and mutual respect, in Jesus' name.

7. Lord, I pray for favor and success in all my endeavors, knowing that You are the ultimate source of blessing and prosperity, in Jesus' name.

8. Father, grant me the strength and perseverance to overcome challenges and obstacles in my career and business pursuits, relying on Your grace and empowerment, in Jesus' name.

9. Lord, I commit my plans and goals to You, seeking Your direction and blessing in every step I take, in Jesus' name.

10. Father, I thank You for the talents and abilities You have bestowed upon me, and I ask for Your anointing to excel in my profession and business endeavors, in Jesus' name.

11. Lord, I pray for divine alignment with Your purposes and plans for my career and business, surrendering my ambitions to Your sovereign will, in Jesus' name.

12. Father, I receive Your blessings of abundance and prosperity with gratitude and humility, knowing that You are the provider of all good things, in Jesus' name.

Affirmation

Father, I affirm today that You are the source of every blessing and success in my career and business. I trust in Your guidance and provision, knowing that You are faithful to fulfill Your promises. May my work be a reflection of Your goodness and grace, bringing glory to Your name and advancing Your kingdom on earth. In Jesus' name, Amen.

Day 7

Prayer for Blessings in Ministry

Ministry is a calling that God entrusts to His people, empowering them to serve others with love, compassion, and grace. Whether it be through preaching, teaching, evangelism, or acts of mercy, every believer is called to participate in God's work of building His kingdom on earth.

In *Matthew 28:19-20*, Jesus commissions His disciples, saying, *"Go therefore and make disciples of all nations, baptizing them in the name of the Father and of the Son and of the Holy Spirit, teaching them to observe all that I have commanded you."* This Great Commission serves as the foundation of Christian ministry, calling us to proclaim the Gospel and make disciples of all people.

Throughout Scripture, we see God's anointing and blessing upon those who faithfully serve Him in ministry. In *Isaiah 61:1-3*, the prophet declares, *"The Spirit of the Lord God is upon me because the Lord has anointed me to bring good news to the poor; he has sent me to bind up the brokenhearted, to proclaim liberty to the captives, and the opening of the prison to those who are bound."*

This passage illustrates God's heart for ministry and His desire to bless His servants with the power and authority to proclaim His truth and bring healing to the nations.

As we come before the Lord in prayer for blessings in ministry today, let us do so with humility, seeking His guidance and empowerment to fulfill His purposes in our lives and in the lives of others.

Prayer Points

1. Heavenly Father, I pray for Your blessings upon my ministry endeavors, that they may be fruitful and effective in advancing Your kingdom on earth, in Jesus' name.

2. Lord, anoint me with Your Holy Spirit, empowering me to preach the Gospel with boldness and clarity, that hearts may be transformed and lives may be saved, in Jesus' name.

3. Father, grant me wisdom and discernment as I minister to others, guiding me in love and compassion to meet their spiritual and practical needs, in Jesus' name.

4. Lord, open doors of opportunity for me to share Your love and truth with those who are lost and hurting, that they may come to know You as their Savior and Lord, in Jesus' name.

5. Father, bless the relationships and partnerships formed through my ministry, that they may be characterized by unity, mutual support, and encouragement, in Jesus' name.

6. Lord, I surrender my plans and ambitions to You, trusting in Your divine guidance and provision for every aspect of my ministry, in Jesus' name.

7. Father, protect me from spiritual attacks and opposition as I engage in ministry, covering me with Your armor and strengthening me in times of trial, in Jesus' name.

8. Lord, grant me the humility to serve others with sincerity and humility, putting their needs above my own and reflecting Your selfless love, in Jesus' name.

9. Father, fill me afresh with Your joy and peace as I labor in Your vineyard, reminding me of the eternal significance of the work You have called me to do, in Jesus' name.

10. Lord, I thank You for the gifts and talents You have given me for ministry, and I ask for Your anointing to use them for Your glory and honor, in Jesus' name.

11. Father, surround me with godly mentors and advisors who can offer guidance and support in my ministry journey, helping me to grow and mature in my faith, in Jesus' name.

12. Lord, I receive Your blessings of abundance and prosperity in ministry with gratitude and humility, knowing that You are the source of every good thing, in Jesus' name.

Affirmation

Heavenly Father, I affirm today that You have called me to be a vessel of Your love and grace in this world. I trust in Your anointing and blessing upon my ministry, knowing that You are faithful to fulfill Your purposes through me. May I walk in obedience and humility, serving others with joy and compassion, and bringing glory to Your name in all that I do. In Jesus' name, Amen.

Day 8

Prayer for Obedience and Blessings

Obedience to God's Word is the pathway to blessings and favor in our lives. In **Deuteronomy 28:1-2**, Moses declares, **"If you fully obey the Lord your God and carefully follow all his commands I give you today, the Lord your God will set you high above all the nations on earth. All these blessings will come on you and accompany you if you obey the Lord your God."** This passage emphasizes the connection between obedience and blessings, highlighting God's desire to pour out His favor upon those who walk in His ways.

Throughout Scripture, we see examples of individuals who experienced the blessings of obedience in their lives. Abraham, Noah, and David are just a few of the many who found favor with God through their obedience and trust in Him. As we seek to live lives that honor and please God, let us come before Him in prayer, asking for the grace and strength to walk in obedience and receive His abundant blessings.

Prayer Points

1. Heavenly Father, I confess that obedience to Your Word is the key to experiencing Your blessings in my life. Help

me to walk in obedience each day, trusting in Your wisdom and guidance, in Jesus' name.

2. Lord, forgive me for the times when I have disobeyed Your commands and gone my own way. Give me a heart of repentance and humility, that I may turn back to You and receive Your forgiveness and restoration, in Jesus' name.

3. Father, grant me the strength and courage to resist temptation and overcome sin, that I may live a life that honors You and reflects Your holiness, in Jesus' name.

4. Lord, teach me to delight in Your Word and meditate on it day and night, that I may be firmly rooted in Your truth and equipped to discern Your will for my life, in Jesus' name.

5. Father, help me to trust in Your promises and obey Your commands even when they seem difficult or contrary to my own desires, knowing that Your ways are higher than my ways, in Jesus' name.

6. Lord, purify my motives and intentions, that I may seek to obey You out of love and devotion rather than fear or selfish ambition, in Jesus' name.

7. Father, surround me with godly influences and accountability partners who will encourage me in my walk of obedience and hold me accountable to Your standards, in Jesus' name.

8. Lord, fill me afresh with Your Holy Spirit, empowering me to obey Your commands and live a life that glorifies You in all that I do, in Jesus' name.

9.   Father, help me to cultivate a spirit of humility and submission, yielding my will to Yours and surrendering all areas of my life to Your lordship, in Jesus' name.

10. Lord, I thank You for the blessings that flow from obedience—blessings of peace, joy, and intimacy with You. May I never take Your grace for granted but continue to walk in obedience all the days of my life, in Jesus' name.

11. Father, guide me in the paths of righteousness and lead me in the way everlasting, that I may experience the fullness of Your blessings and the abundance of Your presence, in Jesus' name.

12. Lord, I receive Your blessings of favor, provision, and protection as I walk in obedience to Your Word, knowing that You are faithful to fulfill Your promises to those who love You, in Jesus' name.

Affirmation

Heavenly Father, I affirm today that obedience to Your Word is the pathway to blessings and favor in my life. I commit myself afresh to walk in Your ways, trusting in Your grace and guidance to lead me each step of the way. May my life be a testimony to Your goodness and faithfulness, as I seek to honor and obey You in all things. In Jesus' name, Amen.

Day 9

Prayer for Abundance
Through Giving

In Luke 6:38, Jesus teaches us, *"Give, and it will be given to you. A good measure, pressed down, shaken together and running over, will be poured into your lap. For with the measure you use, it will be measured to you."* This profound statement reveals the principle of abundance through giving. When we give generously and cheerfully, we open ourselves up to receive blessings beyond measure from the hand of our generous God.

Throughout Scripture, we see examples of individuals and communities experiencing God's abundant provision as a result of their faithful giving. From the widow who gave her last mite to the early church in Acts, the act of giving has always been met with God's abundance and provision.

As we come before the Lord in prayer, let us ask for the grace to cultivate a generous and giving heart, trusting in God's promise to bless us abundantly as we give to others in need.

Prayer Points

1. Heavenly Father, I thank You for Your abundant blessings in my life. Help me to recognize that all that I have comes

from You, and may I steward it well for Your glory, in Jesus' name.

2. Lord, forgive me for any selfishness or greed that has hindered me from giving generously to others. Teach me to be cheerful and willing to share with those in need, in Jesus' name.

3. Father, open my eyes to see the opportunities around me to bless others through giving. Give me a spirit of compassion and generosity, that I may be a channel of Your love and provision to those who are hurting, in Jesus' name.

4. Lord, I surrender my finances and resources to You, trusting that as I give freely, You will pour out Your blessings upon me in abundance, according to Your promise, in Jesus' name.

5. Father, help me to give sacrificially, not out of obligation or compulsion, but out of a sincere desire to bless others and honor You with all that I have, in Jesus' name.

6. Lord, grant me wisdom and discernment in how I give, that I may sow into good soil and reap a harvest of blessings that glorify Your name, in Jesus' name.

7. Father, bless the work of my hands and the fruit of my labor, that I may have an abundance to give to those in need and advance Your kingdom on earth, in Jesus' name.

8. Lord, show me ways to partner with organizations and ministries that are making a difference in the lives of the poor and marginalized, that together we may bring hope and transformation to those in need, in Jesus' name.

9. Father, break any spirit of greed or covetousness that seeks to hold me back from giving generously. Fill me with Your Spirit of generosity and abundance, that I may freely give as You have freely given to me, in Jesus' name.

10. Lord, I declare that I am blessed to be a blessing. May my life be a testimony to Your goodness and provision as I give generously and joyfully to others, in Jesus' name.

11. Father, open the windows of heaven and pour out Your blessings upon me as I walk in obedience to Your command to give. May Your provision overflow in my life and bring glory to Your name, in Jesus' name.

12. Lord, I receive Your promise of abundance through giving and trust that You will supply all my needs according to Your riches in glory, as I continue to honor You with my giving, in Jesus' name.

Affirmation

Heavenly Father, I affirm today that You are the source of all abundance and provision in my life. I commit myself afresh to be a cheerful and generous giver, trusting in Your promise to bless me abundantly as I give to others in need. May my life be a reflection of Your love and generosity, as I seek to bless others and advance Your kingdom on earth. In Jesus' name, Amen.

Day 10

Prayer for Blessings in Community

In *Psalm 133:1*, it is written, *"Behold, how good and how pleasant it is for brethren to dwell together in unity!"* This verse encapsulates the beauty and power of community. God designed us to live in fellowship with one another, supporting, encouraging, and uplifting each other in love.

As we journey through life, we are called to be part of various communities—our families, churches, neighborhoods, workplaces, and beyond. In each of these settings, God desires to pour out His blessings, fostering unity, harmony, and mutual care among His people.

Let us come together in prayer, lifting up our communities before the Lord, and asking for His blessings to abound in our relationships, interactions, and endeavors together.

Prayer Points

1. Gracious Father, we thank You for the gift of community and the relationships that enrich our lives. Bless our communities, Lord, with Your presence, unity, and love, in Jesus' name.

2. Lord, we confess any divisions, strife, or discord that may exist within our communities. Bring healing and

reconciliation, Lord, and help us to walk in humility, gentleness, and patience toward one another, in Jesus' name.

3. Heavenly Father, pour out Your Spirit of unity upon us, that we may be of one mind and one accord, serving and supporting one another with love and grace, in Jesus' name.

4. Lord, bless the leaders and influencers within our communities with wisdom, discernment, and servant hearts. May they lead with integrity, humility, and compassion, seeking the common good and the flourishing of all, in Jesus' name.

5. Father, grant us grace to bear one another's burdens and to rejoice with those who rejoice. Help us to be quick to forgive, slow to anger, and abounding in love toward one another, in Jesus' name.

6. Lord, open our eyes to the needs of those around us within our communities. Give us compassionate hearts and willing hands to serve and minister to the hurting, the marginalized, and the vulnerable, in Jesus' name.

7. Heavenly Father, bless our gatherings, meetings, and interactions within our communities with Your presence and favor. May they be times of encouragement, edification, and spiritual growth, in Jesus' name.

8. Lord, empower us to be agents of positive change and transformation within our communities, shining Your light and spreading Your love wherever we go, in Jesus' name.

9. Father, help us to cultivate an environment of inclusivity, diversity, and respect within our communities, embracing

the unique gifts, talents, and perspectives of each member, in Jesus' name.

10. Lord, strengthen the bonds of friendship and fellowship among us, that we may build each other up and spur one another on toward love and good deeds, in Jesus' name.

11. Gracious God, bless the families within our communities with unity, harmony, and peace. May our homes be havens of love, acceptance, and support, reflecting Your heart for family and community, in Jesus' name.

12. Heavenly Father, we pray for the expansion and multiplication of our communities, that Your kingdom may come and Your will be done on earth as it is in heaven. May our communities be beacons of hope, love, and transformation in a world in need of Your light, in Jesus' name.

Affirmation

Heavenly Father, we affirm today Your desire for us to dwell together in unity and love within our communities. Strengthen us, Lord, to be agents of Your peace, reconciliation, and blessing wherever You have placed us. May our communities be marked by Your presence, grace, and favor, bringing glory to Your name and advancing Your kingdom on earth. In Jesus' name, Amen.

Day 11

Prayer for Protection and Blessing

In a world filled with uncertainties and dangers, seeking God's protection is a natural response for believers. The Bible assures us of God's unfailing love and His promise to watch over His children. *Psalm 91:1-2* declares, *"Whoever dwells in the shelter of the Most High will rest in the shadow of the Almighty. I will say of the Lord, 'He is my refuge and my fortress, my God, in whom I trust.'"*

As we navigate through life's challenges, we can find comfort and strength in knowing that God is our protector and shield. Through prayer, we can seek His divine covering over every aspect of our lives, trusting in His power to keep us safe from harm and to bless us abundantly.

Prayer Points

1. Heavenly Father, we come before You today, acknowledging Your sovereignty and power over all creation. We ask for Your divine protection to surround us like a shield, guarding us from every threat and danger, in Jesus' name.

2. Lord, we pray for Your angels to encamp around us, to deliver us from all evil and to keep us safe in all our ways, according to Your promise in Psalm 34:7, in Jesus' name.

3. Gracious God, we plead the blood of Jesus over our lives, families, and possessions, knowing that it is a powerful weapon against the enemy's schemes. Protect us, Lord, from every form of spiritual attack and oppression, in Jesus' name.

4. Father, shield us from sickness, disease, and infirmity, and grant us divine health and strength to fulfill Your purposes for our lives, in Jesus' name.

5. Lord, we pray for Your divine wisdom and discernment to guide us in making decisions that honor You and align with Your will. Protect us from deception and lead us in paths of righteousness for Your name's sake, in Jesus' name.

6. Heavenly Father, we lift up our loved ones and ask for Your protective hand to be upon them wherever they go. Keep them safe from accidents, harm, and evil influences, covering them with Your grace and mercy, in Jesus' name.

7. Lord, we pray for the protection of our minds and hearts, guarding us against fear, anxiety, and doubt. Fill us with Your peace that surpasses all understanding, anchoring our souls in Your love and truth, in Jesus' name.

8. Gracious God, we ask for Your protection over our homes, sanctuaries of peace and refuge. Let Your presence dwell richly within our households, driving out every force of darkness and establishing an atmosphere of love, unity, and blessing, in Jesus' name.

9. Father, we pray for Your protection over our finances and resources, guarding them from theft, loss, and destruction. Open the windows of heaven and pour out Your blessings upon us, that we may be abundantly

provided for and able to bless others in return, in Jesus' name.

10. Lord, protect our relationships—marriages, friendships, and partnerships—from strife, division, and betrayal. Bind us together in love and harmony, strengthening the bonds of unity and mutual respect, in Jesus' name.

11. Heavenly Father, we pray for Your protection over our nation, leaders, and communities, preserving us from harm and calamity. Let Your peace reign in our land, and may righteousness and justice prevail, in Jesus' name.

12. Lord, we thank You for the assurance of Your constant presence and protection in our lives. Help us to walk in faith and confidence, knowing that You are always with us, keeping us safe and secure in Your unfailing love, in Jesus' name.

Affirmation

Heavenly Father, we affirm today Your faithfulness and goodness toward us, acknowledging You as our protector and shield. Thank You for Your promise to watch over us and keep us safe from harm. We declare Your blessings of protection and favor over our lives, families, and endeavors, trusting in Your unfailing love and care. In Jesus' name, Amen.

Day 12

Prayer for Covenant Blessings

The concept of covenant runs deep within the tapestry of human history and divine purpose. From the earliest pages of Scripture, we see God establishing covenants with His people, promising blessings to those who walk in obedience and faithfulness. In *Genesis 12:2-3*, God made a covenant with Abraham, saying, *"I will make you into a great nation, and I will bless you; I will make your name great, and you will be a blessing. I will bless those who bless you, and whoever curses you I will curse, and all peoples on earth will be blessed through you."*

Throughout the Old Testament, we witness the unfolding of God's covenant relationship with Israel, a people chosen to be a light to the nations. Despite their shortcomings and failures, God remained faithful to His promises, bestowing blessings upon them when they walked in obedience and repentance.

In the New Testament, Jesus inaugurated a new covenant through His sacrificial death and resurrection, offering forgiveness of sins and eternal life to all who believe in Him. As believers in Christ, we are heirs of this new covenant, entitled to its blessings and privileges.

Prayer Points

1. Heavenly Father, we thank You for the covenant of blessings established through Your Son, Jesus Christ. We come before You today, claiming the promises of Your Word and asking You to pour out Your blessings upon us, in Jesus' name.

2. Lord, we repent of any disobedience or unfaithfulness that has hindered Your blessings in our lives. Forgive us, O God, and cleanse us from all unrighteousness, that we may walk blamelessly before You and receive Your covenant blessings, in Jesus' name.

3. Gracious God, we pray for a deeper understanding of Your covenant promises, that we may walk in faith and confidence, knowing that You are faithful to fulfill all Your Word. Open our eyes to see the riches of Your grace and the abundance of Your blessings available to us, in Jesus' name.

4. Father, we declare Your blessings of provision and abundance over every area of our lives—spiritual, emotional, physical, and material. You are our provider and sustainer, and we trust in Your faithfulness to meet all our needs according to Your riches in glory, in Jesus' name.

5. Lord, we pray for Your blessings of peace and joy to fill our hearts and minds, even in the midst of trials and tribulations. Let Your presence be our constant companion, guiding us through every storm and leading us into paths of righteousness, in Jesus' name.

6. Heavenly Father, we pray for Your blessings of favor and success in all our endeavors. May Your hand of blessing

be upon us, prospering the work of our hands and making us a blessing to others, in Jesus' name.

7. Lord, we lift up our families and loved ones to You, asking for Your covenant blessings to rest upon them. Protect them, O God, and keep them safe from harm, sickness, and evil, covering them with Your grace and mercy, in Jesus' name.

8. Gracious God, we pray for Your blessings of wisdom and discernment, that we may make wise choices and follow Your leading in every area of our lives. Help us to walk in obedience and humility, submitting ourselves to Your will and purposes, in Jesus' name.

9. Father, we pray for Your blessings of unity and reconciliation in our relationships. Heal broken hearts and restore what has been lost, bringing reconciliation and peace where there is strife and division, in Jesus' name.

10. Lord, we pray for Your blessings of spiritual growth and maturity, that we may grow in grace and in the knowledge of Your Son, Jesus Christ. Strengthen our faith, O God, and deepen our intimacy with You, that we may bear fruit that will last for eternity, in Jesus' name.

11. Heavenly Father, we pray for Your blessings of protection and provision over Your church, the body of Christ. Empower Your people to be salt and light in the world, proclaiming the good news of salvation and making disciples of all nations, in Jesus' name.

12. Lord, we thank You for the assurance of Your covenant blessings in our lives. May we walk in faith and obedience,

trusting in Your unfailing love and faithfulness to fulfill all Your promises to us, in Jesus' name.

Affirmation

Heavenly Father, we affirm today Your faithfulness and goodness toward us, acknowledging You as our covenant-keeping God. Thank You for Your promises of blessings and favor, which are yes and amen in Christ Jesus. We declare Your covenant blessings over our lives, families, and communities, believing that You are able to do exceedingly abundantly above all that we ask or think. In Jesus' name, Amen.

Day 13

Prayer for Inner Peace and Blessings

In a world filled with chaos and uncertainty, inner peace seems like a distant dream for many. Yet, as believers, we have access to a source of peace that surpasses all understanding. Jesus Himself said in *John 14:27, "Peace I leave with you; my peace I give you. I do not give to you as the world gives. Do not let your hearts be troubled and do not be afraid."*

Inner peace is not merely the absence of turmoil but a deep-seated assurance of God's presence and sovereignty in our lives. It is a fruit of the Spirit, cultivated through prayer, meditation on God's Word, and surrender to His will. *Psalm 29:11* reminds us, *"The Lord gives strength to his people; the Lord blesses his people with peace."*

As we lift our hearts in prayer for inner peace, let us trust in the promises of God to bless us with His peace that guards our hearts and minds in Christ Jesus *(Philippians 4:7)*. Let us surrender our anxieties and fears to Him, knowing that He cares for us *(1 Peter 5:7)* and will grant us the peace that transcends all understanding.

Prayer Points

1. Heavenly Father, I pray for Your blessing of inner peace to flood my soul. Quiet the storms of doubt and fear within me, and fill me with Your perfect peace that surpasses all understanding, in Jesus' name.

2. Lord, I surrender my worries and anxieties to You, knowing that You are my refuge and strength, a very present help in trouble. Bless me with Your peace that calms my troubled heart and mind, in Jesus' name.

3. Gracious God, I pray for Your blessing of serenity amidst the chaos of life. Help me to rest in Your love and trust in Your faithfulness, knowing that You are in control of all things, in Jesus' name.

4. Father, I ask for Your blessing of emotional healing and restoration. Heal the wounds of the past and bring wholeness to every broken area of my life, filling me with Your peace that surpasses all understanding, in Jesus' name.

5. Lord, I pray for Your blessing of clarity and discernment in the midst of confusion. Guide my steps and illuminate Your path before me, that I may walk in Your peace and purpose, in Jesus' name.

6. Heavenly Father, I lift up those who are struggling with anxiety and depression. Pour out Your healing and comforting presence upon them, granting them Your peace that transcends all understanding, in Jesus' name.

7. Lord, I pray for Your blessing of reconciliation and harmony in relationships. Heal broken hearts and mend

fractured bonds, filling us with Your peace and forgiveness, in Jesus' name.

8. Gracious God, I ask for Your blessing of resilience and strength in times of adversity. Help me to stand firm in my faith and trust in Your promises, knowing that You are with me always, in Jesus' name.

9. Father, I pray for Your blessing of rest and refreshment for my soul. Renew my spirit and rejuvenate my mind, that I may find true rest in Your presence, in Jesus' name.

10. Lord, I commit my worries and cares to You, casting all my anxiety on You because You care for me. Bless me with Your peace that guards my heart and mind in Christ Jesus, in Jesus' name.

11. Heavenly Father, I pray for Your blessing of contentment and gratitude in all circumstances. Teach me to be thankful for Your blessings and to find joy in Your presence, no matter the situation, in Jesus' name.

12. Lord, I thank You for Your promise to never leave me nor forsake me. Bless me with the assurance of Your presence and the peace that comes from knowing You, in Jesus' name.

Affirmation

Heavenly Father, I affirm today Your promise to bless me with inner peace that transcends all understanding. I declare that Your peace guards my heart and mind in Christ Jesus, keeping me grounded in Your love and faithfulness. Thank You, Lord, for Your blessings of peace and serenity, which are mine to claim by faith. In Jesus' name, Amen.

Day 14

Prayer for Restoring Broken Blessings

Life is often marked by seasons of brokenness—broken relationships, broken dreams, broken health, and broken spirits. Yet, as believers, we serve a God of restoration and redemption. *Joel 2:25* assures us, *"I will restore to you the years that the swarming locust has eaten, the hopper, the destroyer, and the cutter, my great army, which I sent among you."*

When we face brokenness in our lives, whether caused by our own mistakes or the actions of others, we can turn to God in prayer with confidence, knowing that He is able to heal and restore what is broken. *Psalm 147:3* declares, *"He heals the brokenhearted and binds up their wounds."*

As we lift our hearts in prayer for the restoration of broken blessings, let us trust in God's promise to work all things together for our good *(Romans 8:28)*. Let us surrender our brokenness to Him and believe in His power to bring beauty from ashes and joy from mourning *(Isaiah 61:3)*.

Prayer Points

1. Heavenly Father, I pray for Your blessing of restoration in every area of my life where brokenness has taken hold.

Heal my broken heart, restore my shattered dreams, and redeem what the enemy has stolen, in Jesus' name.

2. Lord, I surrender to You the broken relationships in my life. Heal the wounds of division and discord, and bring reconciliation and forgiveness where there is strife, in Jesus' name.

3. Gracious God, I pray for Your blessing of healing and wholeness in my body. Restore my health and vitality, and strengthen me from the inside out, in Jesus' name.

4. Father, I lift up to You the brokenness in my spirit and soul. Heal the deep-seated wounds of trauma and pain, and renew my mind with Your truth and love, in Jesus' name.

5. Lord, I ask for Your blessing of restoration in my finances and career. Restore what has been lost or stolen, and open doors of opportunity and abundance, in Jesus' name.

6. Heavenly Father, I pray for Your blessing of restoration in my family. Mend broken bonds, heal rifts between loved ones, and bring unity and peace to our home, in Jesus' name.

7. Lord, I commit to You the broken dreams and aspirations of my heart. Restore my hope and vision for the future, and guide me into the plans and purposes You have for me, in Jesus' name.

8. Gracious God, I pray for Your blessing of renewal and revival in my spiritual life. Restore the joy of my salvation, ignite a passion for Your presence, and lead me into deeper intimacy with You, in Jesus' name.

9. Father, I ask for Your blessing of reconciliation and restoration in my community. Heal divisions and injustices, and unite us in love and solidarity, in Jesus' name.

10. Lord, I surrender to You the broken pieces of my past. Redeem my failures and mistakes, and use them for Your glory and my good, in Jesus' name.

11. Heavenly Father, I thank You for Your promise to restore what has been broken in my life. I declare by faith that You are able to do exceedingly abundantly above all that I ask or think, according to Your power that works within me, in Jesus' name.

12. Lord, I receive Your blessing of restoration with gratitude and expectation. I believe that You are faithful to fulfill Your promises, and I trust in Your perfect timing and provision, in Jesus' name.

Affirmation

Heavenly Father, I affirm today Your promise to restore the broken blessings in my life. I declare that You are able to do immeasurably more than all I ask or imagine, according to Your power that is at work within me. Thank You, Lord, for Your faithfulness and grace, which restore and renew me each day. In Jesus' name, Amen.

Day 15

Prayer for Wisdom and Guidance Blessings

In every aspect of our lives, we need wisdom and guidance to navigate the complexities of this world. *Proverbs 4:6-7* reminds us, *"Do not forsake wisdom, and she will protect you; love her, and she will watch over you. The beginning of wisdom is this: Get wisdom. Though it cost all you have, get understanding."*

As we seek God's wisdom and guidance, we acknowledge our dependence on Him, knowing that He alone holds the answers to life's questions and dilemmas. *James 1:5* assures us, *"If any of you lacks wisdom, let him ask God, who gives generously to all without reproach, and it will be given him."*

In prayer, we can bring our concerns, decisions, and uncertainties before the Lord, trusting in His promise to direct our steps and grant us wisdom beyond our own understanding *(Proverbs 3:5-6).* Let us pray fervently for the blessings of wisdom and guidance, knowing that God delights in leading His children along the right path.

Prayer Points

1. Heavenly Father, I pray for Your blessing of wisdom in every area of my life. Grant me discernment to make wise

decisions and insight to understand Your will, in Jesus' name.

2. Lord, I ask for Your guidance as I navigate the challenges and opportunities before me. Lead me in the paths of righteousness and direct my steps according to Your perfect plan, in Jesus' name.

3. Gracious God, I surrender my plans and ambitions to You, trusting in Your wisdom to order my steps. Help me to seek Your guidance in all that I do, and to follow Your leading faithfully, in Jesus' name.

4. Father, I pray for wisdom in my relationships—with family, friends, colleagues, and neighbors. Grant me patience, understanding, and love, that I may reflect Your grace and wisdom in all my interactions, in Jesus' name.

5. Lord, I seek Your wisdom in matters of finance and stewardship. Help me to be wise and faithful with the resources You have entrusted to me, and to use them for Your kingdom purposes, in Jesus' name.

6. Heavenly Father, I ask for Your guidance in my career and vocational pursuits. Open doors of opportunity and align my path with Your perfect will, that I may glorify You in all that I do, in Jesus' name.

7. Lord, I pray for wisdom in times of uncertainty and doubt. Grant me peace and clarity of mind, that I may trust in Your providence and wisdom to guide me through every trial, in Jesus' name.

8. Gracious God, I seek Your wisdom in matters of health and well-being. Grant me wisdom to care for my body, mind, and spirit, and to honor You with my lifestyle choices, in Jesus' name.

9. Father, I pray for wisdom in my spiritual walk. Help me to discern Your voice and to follow Your leading with humility and obedience, knowing that You alone are the source of true wisdom, in Jesus' name.

10. Lord, I ask for Your guidance in my decision-making process. Help me to seek Your will above all else and to trust in Your wisdom to lead me in the right direction, in Jesus' name.

11. Heavenly Father, I thank You for the promise of Your wisdom and guidance in my life. I declare by faith that You are my source of wisdom and understanding, and I trust in Your faithfulness to lead me each day, in Jesus' name.

12. Lord, I receive Your blessings of wisdom and guidance with gratitude and expectation. I believe that You are faithful to fulfill Your promises, and I trust in Your sovereign plan for my life, in Jesus' name.

Affirmation

Heavenly Father, I affirm today Your promise to grant me wisdom and guidance as I seek Your will. I declare that Your wisdom surpasses all understanding, and I trust in Your guidance to lead me in the paths of righteousness. Thank You, Lord, for Your faithfulness and grace, which lead me forward each day. In Jesus' name, Amen.

Day 16

Prayer for Generational Blessings

As we lift our hearts in prayer for generational blessings, we recognize the importance of God's promises extending not only to us but also to our descendants. In *Genesis 12:2-3*, the Lord said to Abram, *"I will make you into a great nation, and I will bless you; I will make your name great, and you will be a blessing. I will bless those who bless you, and whoever curses you I will curse; and all peoples on earth will be blessed through you."*

God's desire to bless extends through generations, encompassing not only our present but also our future. In praying for generational blessings, we acknowledge our role as stewards of God's promises, passing down His blessings to our children and their children after them *(Deuteronomy 6:6-7). These commandments that I give you today are to be on your hearts. Impress them on your children. Talk about them when you sit at home and when you walk along the road, when you lie down and when you get up*

Let us pray fervently for generational blessings, believing that God's promises are yes and amen in Christ Jesus *(2 Corinthians 1:20),* and that His blessings will flow from generation to generation. *"For no matter how many promises God has made, they are "Yes" in Christ. And so through him the "Amen" is spoken by us to the glory of God"*

Prayer Points

1. Heavenly Father, I pray for Your blessings to flow through my family line, from generation to generation. May Your favor rest upon us and Your protection surround us, in Jesus' name.

2. Lord, I ask for Your grace to be upon my children and their children after them. May they walk in Your ways and experience Your blessings in abundance, in Jesus' name.

3. Gracious God, I pray for healing and restoration in my family line. Break every chain of bondage and generational curses, and release Your blessings of freedom and wholeness, in Jesus' name.

4. Father, I lift up my descendants before You, praying for their salvation and spiritual growth. Draw them close to You and reveal Your love and grace to them, that they may live lives that honor and glorify You, in Jesus' name.

5. Lord, I pray for generational blessings in every area of my family's life—spiritual, emotional, physical, and financial. Pour out Your blessings upon us, O Lord, and make us a testimony of Your goodness and faithfulness, in Jesus' name.

6. Heavenly Father, I commit my family line into Your hands, trusting in Your promises to bless and prosper us. May Your presence go before us and Your favor follow us all the days of our lives, in Jesus' name.

7. Lord, I ask for wisdom and discernment to lead my family in the ways of righteousness. Help us to walk in obedience to Your word and to pass down Your truth and values to the next generation, in Jesus' name.

8. Gracious God, I pray for unity and love to abound in my family. May Your peace reign in our hearts, and may we always seek to build one another up in faith and love, in Jesus' name.

9. Father, I pray for generational blessings in the area of provision and abundance. Open the windows of heaven and pour out Your blessings upon us, that we may be a blessing to others, in Jesus' name.

10. Lord, I pray for generational blessings of good health and vitality. Keep us strong and healthy, both in body and in spirit, that we may serve You faithfully all the days of our lives, in Jesus' name.

11. Heavenly Father, I thank You for the promise of generational blessings that You have given to those who love You and walk in Your ways. I declare by faith that Your blessings are upon me and my descendants, and I trust in Your unfailing love and faithfulness, in Jesus' name.

12. Lord, I receive Your generational blessings with gratitude and humility, knowing that You are a God who keeps His promises. May Your name be glorified through the blessings You pour out upon my family line, now and forevermore, in Jesus' name.

Affirmation

Heavenly Father, I affirm today Your promise to bless me and my descendants, according to Your word. I declare that Your blessings are upon us, and we will walk in Your favor and grace all the days of our lives. Thank You, Lord, for Your faithfulness and goodness, which extend from generation to generation. In Jesus' name, Amen.

Day 17

Prayer for Blessings of Gratitude

In a world often overshadowed by uncertainty and unrest, the practice of gratitude emerges as a powerful antidote, illuminating the darkest corners of our hearts with rays of hope and thankfulness. Gratitude is not merely a fleeting emotion but a transformative attitude—a conscious choice to recognize and appreciate the blessings that grace our lives each day.

Scripture abounds with exhortations to cultivate a spirit of gratitude. In *Psalm 100:4*, we are urged to enter His gates with thanksgiving and His courts with praise, acknowledging that the Lord is good and His love endures forever. The Apostle Paul echoes this sentiment in *1 Thessalonians 5:18*, *"...give thanks in all circumstances; for this is God's will for you in Christ Jesus"* instructing us to give thanks in all circumstances, for this is God's will for us in Christ Jesus.

Gratitude is not contingent upon favorable circumstances but transcends them, finding expression even in the midst of trials and tribulations. When we adopt an attitude of gratitude, we shift our focus from what we lack to what we have been given, from our burdens to our blessings. Through gratitude, we discover the hidden treasures of joy, peace, and contentment, which abound in God's abundant provision.

Let us now come together in prayer, seeking the blessings of gratitude to overflow in our hearts and lives, transforming our perspective and infusing each moment with the radiance of God's goodness.

Prayer Points

1. Gracious Father, I thank You for the countless blessings You have bestowed upon me, seen and unseen. Grant me a heart overflowing with gratitude, that I may continually offer praise and thanksgiving to You, in Jesus' name.

2. Lord, help me to cultivate a spirit of gratitude in every circumstance, knowing that You work all things together for my good. May I find joy and contentment in Your provision, trusting in Your unfailing love, in Jesus' name.

3. Heavenly Father, forgive me for the times I have taken Your blessings for granted and failed to express gratitude. Teach me to be mindful of Your goodness and mercy each day, that I may live a life marked by thanksgiving and praise, in Jesus' name.

4. Lord, open my eyes to the abundant blessings that surround me, even in the midst of trials and challenges. Help me to see Your hand at work in every situation, and to respond with a heart full of gratitude, in Jesus' name.

5. Gracious God, I pray for the grace to appreciate the simple joys and blessings of life—the beauty of creation, the love of family and friends, and the gift of each new

day. May gratitude be the melody of my soul, resonating with Your love and goodness, in Jesus' name.

6. Heavenly Father, I lift up those who are struggling to find reasons to be grateful, weighed down by sorrow, pain, or loss. Pour out Your comfort and peace upon them, and remind them of Your unchanging love and faithfulness, in Jesus' name.

7. Lord, help me to be a conduit of Your blessings, sharing Your love and kindness with others. May my life be a reflection of Your grace and mercy, drawing others to You through acts of generosity and compassion, in Jesus' name.

8. Gracious God, I pray for a spirit of thankfulness to permeate every aspect of my life—my thoughts, words, and actions. May gratitude be my constant companion, guiding me closer to You and Your perfect will, in Jesus' name.

9. Lord, I thank You for the gift of salvation through Your Son, Jesus Christ, and for the hope of eternal life with You. May this greatest of blessings fill me with awe and wonder, inspiring me to live each day for Your glory, in Jesus' name.

10. Heavenly Father, I commit to making gratitude a priority in my life, acknowledging Your goodness and faithfulness at all times. May my heart overflow with thanksgiving, becoming a source of blessing and encouragement to those around me, in Jesus' name.

11. Lord, I pray for a renewed perspective on life, seeing every experience as an opportunity to grow in gratitude and faith. Help me to recognize Your blessings in disguise

and to trust Your perfect timing and plan for my life, in Jesus' name.

12. Gracious God, I thank You for hearing and answering my prayers, according to Your will and Your perfect timing. May Your blessings of gratitude continue to abound in my life, drawing me closer to You and Your purposes, in Jesus' name.

Affirmation

Heavenly Father, I affirm today my commitment to live a life marked by gratitude and praise. I declare that Your blessings of thanksgiving overflow in my heart, transforming my perspective and infusing each moment with the radiance of Your goodness. Thank You, Lord, for Your abundant blessings, which I receive with joy and thanksgiving, in Jesus' name. Amen.

Day 18

Prayer for Blessings in Adversity

In the midst of life's storms and trials, we often find ourselves longing for relief, for an end to the adversity that threatens to overwhelm us. Yet, it is in these very moments of hardship that God's blessings shine most brightly, illuminating the path before us with hope and perseverance.

Scripture assures us that God is with us in the midst of adversity, working all things together for our good *(Romans 8:28)*. *"And we know that in all things God works for the good of those who love him, who have been called according to his purpose."*

"Even though I walk through the darkest valley, I will fear no evil, for you are with me; your rod and your staff, they comfort me". Even when we walk through the darkest valleys, His presence is our comfort and strength *(Psalm 23:4)*.

In *James 1:2-4,* we are encouraged to consider it pure joy when we face trials, knowing that they produce perseverance, character, and hope.

Let us now come together in prayer, trusting in God's promise to bless us even in the midst of adversity. May His grace sustain us, His peace surround us, and His blessings overflow in our lives, no matter what challenges we may face.

Prayer Points

1. Heavenly Father, I thank You for Your promise to never leave me nor forsake me, even in the midst of adversity. Grant me the strength to trust in Your goodness and faithfulness, knowing that Your blessings are greater than any trial I may face, in Jesus' name.

2. Lord, I lift up to You all those who are experiencing adversity and hardship, whether physical, emotional, or spiritual. Pour out Your comfort and peace upon them, and may Your blessings sustain them through every trial, in Jesus' name.

3. Gracious God, forgive me for the times I have allowed adversity to overshadow Your blessings in my life. Help me to see Your hand at work even in the midst of trials, and to trust in Your perfect plan and timing, in Jesus' name.

4. Lord, I pray for the grace to persevere in faithfulness and obedience, even when faced with adversity. May Your blessings of strength and courage enable me to stand firm in Your promises, knowing that You are faithful to fulfill them, in Jesus' name.

5. Heavenly Father, I surrender my fears and anxieties to You, knowing that You are greater than any adversity I

may face. Fill me with Your peace that surpasses understanding, and may Your blessings of hope and assurance sustain me through every storm, in Jesus' name.

6. Lord, I pray for a renewed perspective on adversity, seeing it as an opportunity for growth and spiritual maturity. Help me to embrace the challenges I encounter, knowing that Your blessings abound even in the midst of trials, in Jesus' name.

7. Gracious God, I thank You for the lessons You teach me through adversity, and for the ways You use it to refine and strengthen my faith. Help me to trust in Your sovereignty and goodness, knowing that You are working all things together for my good, in Jesus' name.

8. Lord, I pray for a heart of gratitude in the face of adversity, recognizing Your blessings amidst the storms of life. Help me to focus on Your goodness and faithfulness, rather than dwelling on the challenges before me, in Jesus' name.

9. Heavenly Father, I commit to seeking Your presence and guidance in every trial and difficulty I face. May Your blessings of wisdom and discernment lead me through the darkest valleys, and may Your light shine brightly in the midst of adversity, in Jesus' name.

10. Lord, I pray for the strength to trust in Your promises, even when the storms of life rage around me. Help me to

anchor my hope in Your unchanging love and faithfulness, knowing that Your blessings are sufficient for every need, in Jesus' name.

11. Gracious God, I thank You for Your faithfulness in times of adversity, and for Your promise to never leave me nor forsake me. Help me to cling to Your word and Your presence, knowing that Your blessings sustain me through every trial, in Jesus' name.

12. Lord, I pray for a heart of praise and thanksgiving, even in the midst of adversity. May Your blessings overflow in my life, filling me with joy and peace that surpasses understanding, in Jesus' name.

Affirmation

Heavenly Father, I affirm today my trust in Your goodness and faithfulness, even in the midst of adversity. I declare that Your blessings sustain me, Your peace surrounds me, and Your love upholds me through every trial and difficulty. Thank You, Lord, for Your abundant blessings, which I receive with gratitude and praise, in Jesus' name. Amen.

Day 19

Prayer for Divine Intervention and Blessing

As we journey through life, we encounter situations and challenges that are beyond our control. In those moments, we often find ourselves in desperate need of divine intervention – a miraculous touch from God to bring about change, healing, and breakthrough.

Scripture reminds us that nothing is impossible for our God, and He is always ready to intervene on behalf of His children when they call upon Him in faith.

In Jeremiah 32:27, the Lord declares, *"Behold, I am the Lord, the God of all flesh. Is anything too hard for me?"* This verse reassures us of God's unlimited power and ability to intervene in any situation, no matter how dire it may seem. Similarly, in *Matthew 19:26*, Jesus affirms, *"With man this is impossible, but with God all things are possible."*

Let us now come together in prayer, believing in God's power to intervene in our lives and trusting in His abundant blessings to accompany His divine actions. May we approach the throne of grace with confidence, knowing that our Heavenly Father hears our prayers and delights in blessing His children.

Prayer Points

1. Heavenly Father, I come before You with humility and reverence, acknowledging Your sovereignty and power over all things. I lift up to You the situations in my life that are in need of divine intervention, trusting in Your wisdom and mercy to bring about breakthrough and blessing, in Jesus' name.

2. Lord, I thank You for Your promise to hear and answer the prayers of Your children. I ask for Your divine intervention in every area of my life where I am in need of Your touch – physically, emotionally, spiritually, and financially. May Your blessings overflow as You work miracles on my behalf, in Jesus' name.

3. Gracious God, I surrender my will and my desires to You, trusting in Your perfect plan for my life. Help me to align my prayers with Your purposes, knowing that Your ways are higher than my ways and Your thoughts higher than my thoughts, in Jesus' name.

4. Lord, I pray for divine wisdom and discernment to recognize Your leading and guidance in every situation I face. May Your Holy Spirit empower me to pray according to Your will, confident that You are working all things together for my good, in Jesus' name.

5. Heavenly Father, I lift up to You those who are facing impossible situations and insurmountable challenges. Pour out Your grace and mercy upon them, and may Your divine intervention bring healing, restoration, and blessing beyond measure, in Jesus' name.

6. Lord, I pray for a spirit of faith and expectancy to arise within me as I wait upon You for divine intervention. Help

me to stand firm on Your promises, knowing that You are faithful to fulfill them and that Your blessings are always on time, in Jesus' name.

7. Gracious God, I rebuke every hindrance and obstacle that stands in the way of Your divine intervention in my life. I declare Your victory and authority over every situation, and I claim Your blessings of breakthrough and deliverance, in Jesus' name.

8. Lord, I pray for divine protection and provision as I step out in faith and obedience to Your leading. May Your angels encamp around me, and may Your blessings pave the way for success and victory in every endeavor, in Jesus' name.

9. Heavenly Father, I thank You for the times You have intervened miraculously in my life, bringing about blessings beyond my wildest dreams. I choose to remember Your faithfulness and goodness, and I trust You to continue working miracles in my life, in Jesus' name.

10. Lord, I pray for a heart of gratitude and praise, even in the midst of waiting for Your divine intervention. Help me to trust in Your timing and to rejoice in Your faithfulness, knowing that Your blessings are always worth the wait, in Jesus' name.

11. Gracious God, I pray for divine peace and comfort to fill my heart as I rest in Your promises. May Your presence surround me, and may Your blessings sustain me through every trial and difficulty, in Jesus' name.

12. Lord, I pray for an outpouring of Your Holy Spirit upon Your people, igniting a revival of faith, hope, and love.

May Your blessings flow abundantly, bringing healing, reconciliation, and salvation to all who call upon Your name, in Jesus' name.

Affirmation

Heavenly Father, I affirm today my unwavering trust in Your power and goodness to intervene miraculously in my life. I declare that Your blessings are abundant, Your love is unfailing, and Your grace is more than sufficient for every need. Thank You, Lord, for Your divine intervention and blessings, which I receive with gratitude and praise, in Jesus' name. Amen.

Day 20

Prayer for Abundant Harvest
of Blessings

As we journey through the seasons of life, we sow seeds of faith, hope, and love, trusting in the promise of God's abundant harvest of blessings. Just as a farmer diligently tends to his fields, nurturing the soil and patiently waiting for the fruits of his labor, so too do we cultivate our hearts in prayer, eagerly anticipating the bountiful blessings that God has in store for us.

In *Galatians 6:9*, the Apostle Paul encourages us, *"Let us not become weary in doing good, for at the proper time we will reap a harvest if we do not give up."* This verse reminds us of the importance of perseverance and steadfastness in our walk of faith, knowing that God is faithful to fulfill His promises in His perfect timing.

Let us now come together in prayer, lifting up our hearts to the Lord in expectation of an abundant harvest of blessings. May we sow seeds of kindness, generosity, and compassion, knowing that our Heavenly Father delights in blessing His children beyond measure.

Prayer Points

1. Heavenly Father, I thank You for the promise of an abundant harvest of blessings for those who diligently seek You and obey Your commands. I pray that You would open the floodgates of heaven and pour out Your blessings upon me in abundance, in Jesus' name.

2. Lord, I surrender every area of my life to Your sovereign care and authority, trusting in Your wisdom and goodness to bring about a fruitful harvest of blessings. May Your favor rest upon me, and may Your blessings overflow in every season, in Jesus' name.

3. Gracious God, I pray for a spirit of generosity and gratitude to fill my heart as I await the harvest of blessings You have promised. Help me to sow seeds of faith, hope, and love wherever I go, knowing that You are faithful to bring about an abundant harvest, in Jesus' name.

4. Lord, I pray for divine wisdom and discernment to recognize the opportunities You place before me to sow seeds of blessing in the lives of others. May Your Holy Spirit guide me in sowing generously and reaping bountifully, for Your glory and honor, in Jesus' name.

5. Heavenly Father, I lift up to You the seeds of prayer that I have sown in faith, trusting in Your power to bring about a mighty harvest of answered prayers. Strengthen my faith, Lord, and help me to persevere in prayer until I see Your blessings manifest in my life, in Jesus' name.

6. Lord, I pray for a heart that is sensitive to Your leading and obedient to Your will. May I be willing to step out in faith and sow seeds of blessing even when it seems

impractical or risky, knowing that You are able to do immeasurably more than all we ask or imagine, according to Your power that is at work within us, in Jesus' name.

7. Gracious God, I rebuke every spirit of doubt, fear, and unbelief that would hinder me from sowing and reaping Your blessings in my life. I declare Your promises over every area of my life, believing that You are faithful to fulfill them, in Jesus' name.

8. Lord, I pray for a heart that is quick to repent and seek Your forgiveness when I fail to sow seeds of blessing or when I allow sin to take root in my life. Create in me a clean heart, O God, and renew a steadfast spirit within me, that I may continue to sow and reap Your blessings, in Jesus' name.

9. Heavenly Father, I thank You for the times You have already blessed me with an abundant harvest of blessings, far beyond what I could ask or imagine. I choose to remember Your faithfulness and goodness, and I trust You to continue to bless me abundantly in the days to come, in Jesus' name.

10. Lord, I pray for a spirit of humility and gratitude to accompany the harvest of blessings You pour out upon me. Help me to steward Your blessings well and to use them for Your glory and the advancement of Your kingdom, in Jesus' name.

11. Gracious God, I pray for a multiplication of blessings in every area of my life – spiritually, physically, financially, and relationally. May Your blessings overflow and touch the lives of those around me, bringing glory to Your name, in Jesus' name.

12. Lord, I pray for an attitude of expectancy and faith as I wait for the harvest of blessings You have promised. Help me to stand firm on Your word and to trust in Your faithfulness, knowing that You are able to do far more abundantly than all that I ask or think, according to the power at work within me, in Jesus' name.

Affirmation

Heavenly Father, I affirm today my unwavering trust in Your promise of an abundant harvest of blessings. I declare that Your blessings are already on their way, and I receive them with gratitude and praise, knowing that You are faithful to fulfill Your promises to those who believe. Thank You, Lord, for Your faithfulness and goodness, which I receive with open hands and a grateful heart, in Jesus' name. Amen.

Day 21

Prayer for Overflowing Blessings of Love

Love is the golden thread that binds us together, weaving its way through every aspect of our existence. It is the foundation upon which all other blessings are built, the essence of our humanity, and the greatest gift we have been given by our Heavenly Father. As we gather in prayer today, let us open our hearts to receive the overflowing blessings of love that God longs to pour out upon us.

The Bible tells us in *1 Corinthians 13:13, "And now these three remain: faith, hope, and love. But the greatest of these is love."* This powerful scripture reminds us of the supremacy of love in the kingdom of God, highlighting its eternal significance and unmatched value. Love is not merely a fleeting emotion or a temporary feeling; it is an enduring force that transcends time and space, transforming lives and renewing hearts.

As we embark on this journey of prayer, let us fix our eyes on the source of all love, our Heavenly Father, who loved us so much that He sent His only Son to die for our sins. Let us pray with faith and expectation, knowing that God delights in blessing His children with an abundance of love, grace, and mercy. May our hearts overflow with love for God and for one another, as we experience the fullness of His blessings in our lives.

Prayer Points

1. Heavenly Father, I thank You for Your unfailing love that surrounds me like a shield, protecting me from harm and guiding me along the path of righteousness. I pray that Your love would overflow in my heart and pour out onto those around me, blessing them with Your grace and compassion, in Jesus' name.

2. Lord, I pray for a deeper revelation of Your love for me, that I may fully comprehend the height, depth, and breadth of Your great love. Help me to experience Your love in tangible ways, filling every empty space in my heart and renewing my mind with Your truth, in Jesus' name.

3. Gracious God, I surrender my fears, doubts, and insecurities to You, knowing that Your perfect love casts out all fear. I pray that Your love would cast out every trace of anxiety and uncertainty from my life, replacing them with peace and confidence in Your promises, in Jesus' name.

4. Lord, I pray for the strength to love others as You have loved me – unconditionally, sacrificially, and without reservation. Help me to extend grace, forgiveness, and compassion to those who need it most, reflecting Your love to a world that is in desperate need of Your light, in Jesus' name.

5. Heavenly Father, I pray for healing and restoration in relationships that have been broken or strained by

conflict, misunderstanding, or betrayal. Pour out Your love and reconciliation upon us, Lord, that we may experience the joy of unity and harmony once again, in Jesus' name.

6. Lord, I pray for marriages and families to be strengthened and united by Your love, as husbands and wives, parents and children, brothers and sisters, commit to loving one another as You have loved us. May Your love be the glue that holds us together through every trial and triumph, in Jesus' name.

7. Gracious God, I pray for the lonely, the brokenhearted, and the outcast, that they may experience the transformative power of Your love in their lives. Wrap them in Your loving embrace, Lord, and remind them that they are cherished and valued beyond measure, in Jesus' name.

8. Lord, I pray for the courage to love my enemies and to bless those who curse me, knowing that Your love has the power to overcome evil with good. Help me to extend grace and forgiveness to those who have wronged me, and to pray for their salvation and redemption, in Jesus' name.

9. Heavenly Father, I pray for a spirit of unity and harmony to permeate Your church, as believers come together in love and fellowship, to worship You in spirit and in truth. May Your love be a beacon of hope and reconciliation in a world that is divided and broken, in Jesus' name.

10. Lord, I pray for an outpouring of Your love upon our communities, cities, and nations, that hearts may be softened and lives transformed by the power of Your love. Use us as instruments of Your love and grace, Lord,

to shine Your light into the darkest corners of the world, in Jesus' name.

11. Gracious God, I pray for a revival of love in the hearts of Your people, that we may be known by our love for one another and for You. Help us to love as You have loved us, Lord, that Your name may be glorified and Your kingdom advanced in the earth, in Jesus' name.

12. Lord, I pray for an overflow of Your love in every area of my life – in my relationships, my work, my ministry, and my everyday interactions. May Your love be the driving force behind everything I say and do, bringing glory and honor to Your name, in Jesus' name.

Affirmation

Heavenly Father, I affirm today my unwavering trust in Your promise of overflowing blessings of love. I declare that Your love never fails, never gives up, and never runs out on me. Thank You, Lord, for filling my heart to overflowing with Your love, grace, and mercy, which I receive with joy and gratitude, in Jesus' name. Amen.

Made in United States
Troutdale, OR
02/05/2025